harmony

Reverend Henry C. Frascadore

Copyright

ALSO BY REVEREND HENRY C. FRASCADORE

conversations after sunset

Beyond the Weeping Willow Tree
. . . Mystery is a Gift Wrapped in Ordinary Paper

Foreword

Harmony is the brilliant culmination of a trilogy of inspired poetic collections of Fr. Henry C. Frascadore, written during the retirement years of this exceptionally gifted Catholic priest following his more than half a century of devoted service.

In his elegant style of poetic simplicity, *Harmony* and his earlier collections, *Beyond the Weeping Willow Tree*, (2011), and *Conversations After Sunset,* (2013), emerge as delightful, yet deeply moving poetry that opens hearts and minds to a new sense of significance of each and every member of God's universe.

No introductory words can match the rich rewards of reading *Harmony* itself, verse by verse, recounting the adventures and observations of the lively daily walks of the author and his devoted canine companion, Ramsey. Together, they observe, inspect, (sniff, in Ramsey's case), and reflect on all that they see on the city streets: the regulars walking to the bus stop and those coming off the bus; the occasional stranger; the park with its oak, elm and even an ugly pine tree; the welcome crocus, robin and splashing sounds of a fountain in early spring; the pond with its goldfish, eleven ducks sitting on the pond's edge and the heron lurking patiently in a nearby branch of a tree. The chronicled passages of man and dog are joyfully interspersed with stories of the parables and good news of the Gospel of Jesus, reaching beyond the credible to the miracles of faith.

The descriptions of the sights, sounds and sensations of the wind, rain, a snowflake, a roaring wave or the waxing and waning of the moon arouse renewed appreciation of nature, thus awakening us to the presence of God as we notice a squirrel stepping on a fallen twig, a soaring eagle and the special place of every other member of creation on our magnificent planet.

In the final analysis, the sheer beauty of *Harmony* stands on its own, allowing each of us to be drawn to our own particular insights, leaving no need for further introduction beyond the enlightening experience of turning each page of a visionary's exquisite artistry.

E. Richard Fortunato

E. Richard Fortunato is a retired senior marketing officer of an internationally recognized manufacturer of fine timepieces. The focus of his 20 years of retirement in Southington, CT, has been to try to live his faith in action through service to his church and the wider community using his organizational skills and his passion for writing to promote the work of the community's non-profits serving the poor, the hungry, the homeless, the aging, our veterans and the healthy development and education of our youth.

harmony

table of contents

ascension

just because i said
that i am going to the Father
i don't want you standing around
looking up at the heavens
waiting for me to appear from among the clouds

i told you the other day
that i never would leave you
i'd be always at your side

so rather than risk a stiff neck by looking up
look around you
at the people across from you at the supper table
or standing ahead of you
in the express lane of the supermarket
with a bagful of coupons

as unlikely as this may sound
that is where i am
next to you and around you
and in you

a boy of five asked me after Mass one Sunday
how do i get to heaven
i told him to walk holding hands with Jesus
he said
no
i mean what road do i take

why is it that we make holiness so difficult

bam

I met Dorothy entering the park
       from Trinity Street early this morning.
We've met there before.
She's the one who told me
       that her husband's name was Henry.
I wisecracked and asked
       what is it now.
She thought and said
       probably the same.
She still helps out in the morning at a shelter.
       When I met her two years ago it was at a shelter in
          East Hartford.
       Now it's at the one on Park Street in Hartford.
She takes a bus from the north end
       to Union Station
       and then walks across the park to work.
She doesn't get paid for the work she does.
It's her way of helping others.
She's been doing it for years
       ever since her husband died seven years ago.
She's seventy-one
       has a terrible back problem
       and finds it hard to walk.
But she wants to do what she does.
She thinks that the world is all mixed up
       poor and hungry people
       guns and drugs.
She told me that
       Henry used to say the Our Father
       every morning standing in the backyard
       looking up to heaven.
I could bash him in the nose
       she said.
Your husband
       I said.

No the Father.
He hasn't done a thing about the mess we're in.
She repeated what she said before
      but this time she clenched her fist like Willie Pep
      cocked her arm
      looked up to heaven
         and said in full voice "BAM!"

be awake when the moment comes

Jesus says "Stay awake."
Being awake when the moment comes
he says
is crucial.
It comes and goes quickly.
There are no warnings no alarms
            no shakes of the shoulder to arouse you.
It comes at a time you don't expect.
And what it holds is anyone's guess.

I was walking through the mall last week
looking for the AT&T store
when a student stopped me and asked
"Do you remember me?"
"Yes."
And when I said his name
he smiled.
He knew I knew him.
"Do you remember" he said "when I told you
            that I no longer believed in God
            and what you said to me?"
"Yes" I said "but God still believes in you."
"Thank you for saying that" he said
            "then and now."

bread alone

On a Sunday afternoon
after a big meal
and a glass of red wine

we're not inclined to think
of the challenges
yet to be met

We're happy to rest
close our eyes
and wait for the PGA to start

Isn't that the good life
tilt back the recliner
and beckon Morpheus to do his thing

But Jesus said it's not by bread alone we live
but on every word that comes
from the mouth of God

This morning God's words
came from the gnarled mouth
of an ancient elm tree

It said just because your stomachs
are full don't think
that everyone's are

We must think about that
before we call on Morpheus
to do his thing

breaking the law

lepers were disliked from a distance
they were unclean
contagious filthy and smelly
even their families disliked them
lepers lived on the edge of life
the only ones with whom they spoke
were other lepers

a leper saw Jesus
come down from the mountain
and took the chance of breaking the law
ran up to him
fell to his knees
and begged for cleanliness
Jesus broke the law and touched him

two people breaking the law
one out of trust
the other out of love

Brother Sun and Sister Moon

The father of Francis was a wealthy merchant
lived accordingly
and expected that his son
would do the same.

But Francis wasn't into fine wines and fancy clothes
he chose to walk with the poor
which cost him his inheritance.
In its place were
the limitless treasures of the universe
which he packaged in words
and freely gave to those in need.

No one remembers the silk robes
his father designed and sold at great price
to the rich in Assisi
but everyone remembers "Brother Sun and Sister Moon."

Cape Cod

I am at the seashore
waiting for the sun to rise.
Wrapped around the horizon
is a wide band of deep red.
The sky is clear,
the bay is still.

I am sitting next to a man
who sees what I see
and is writing,
> "The Lord's voice resounding on the waters
> the Lord on the immensity of the waters
> the voice of the Lord full of power
> the voice of the Lord full of splendor . . . .
> The Lord's voice flashes flames of fire."

He too got here early
to catch the dawn
for dawn is the usual time
to meet the Spirit.

What a wonderful experience
for me on the brink of sunrise
to be next to the man
who thousands of years ago
sat here by the sea
seeing the same thing we are beholding together
and allowing me
to get into his head
and share his feelings.

Each day has its own beginning
but some are more wonderful than others
and this is one of them.

chisel

early mornings in the park make me think
that's enough to make me grateful
to get up and think
what a blessing

there are noises at six
of course
the traffic and the birds' songs
and the greetings of those on the way to work

one of the things
i think about is
how difficult thinking is
i mean thinking about something to say

i think about the trees
which i see in the park every day
i know where they are and what they are called
i am interested in them

some are old and failing terribly
the oriental twin oak
on the way to the Capitol Building
hasn't much time left

and the big white oak
on the edge of the lily pond
is dying by inches
the trunk is rotting

and i think about Ramsey
and wonder what he is thinking about
does he know that he's
getting older and slowing down

and once that happens
my thoughts race down
sad highways
highways i wish weren't there

and of course
early in the morning
are thoughts about God
and why things are so confusing

why couldn't our thoughts
be like finches flying through
the branches of trees
and bumping into none of them

they make it look so easy
they get something into their heads
then off at full speed
in search of whatever they had in mind

we on the other hand
pick up a hammer and chisel
and start chipping away
at solid marble

hoping that if we keep chiseling
a face will appear
a beautiful face that
speaks without words

dance a new dance

dance a new dance for the Lord
as the linden trees and the marigolds do
every day it rains

they step and move
in different ways
to the rhythm of the rain

they're aware
that while some think rain is rain and wind is wind
they know differently

they know a drizzle from a downpour
a zephyr from a gale
and dance accordingly

this afternoon at four
they performed a riotous ballet
not a languorous waltz

in gratitude for the tumultuous way
the Lord
changed the late day's scenery

leave it to trees and flowers
to remind us of
what we often miss--

we are all in this together
and
life is one and life is holy

whatever's living becomes us
if we but take
time to welcome it

danced to heavenly music

it is one thing to hear heavenly music
and another to dance to it

and the faithful
in the assembly of Yahweh

heard the music
and danced to it

they rejoiced
and burst into song

with their feet
matching the rhythm

of the timbrels and harps
in a festive dance

declaring their joy
of being Yahweh's chosen ones

to those who slept on couches
and those who did not

joy explodes when shared
and shrivels when it is not

no one knows that better
than those who heard

the music of the heavens and danced to it
for the delight of all

the difference between fear and freedom

this was her moment
she couldn't let it pass
Jesus may not come this way again
if she missed him
      her shame would go on

her fear was trumped
she pushed her way through the crowd
people hissed at her
she didn't hear them

only he was on her mind

now close
      she stretched out her hand
a tassel on his robe hung free
she touched it
      and then his voice

your courage has set you free
you know that moments pass quickly and then are gone
      so you held this one tightly
      which made the difference between fear and
          freedom

dinosaurs in the sky

there were eleven ducks on the pond
this morning at six
and three dinosaurs in the skies
this afternoon at five

don't crush acorns

This morning at six
Jupiter nearly a billion miles away
seems close.

The wind
a yelping cowboy
is driving herds of leaves
across the western plains.

Ice covers most of the pond
and the fountain is struggling
to spout one last time.

The bushes along Wells Street are bare
and Ramsey who loves small leaves to nibble on
is visibly disappointed.

"Things change"
I say to him.
He ignores my wisdom.

We keep walking.
Beneath my boots
I can hear acorns crunching
and I wonder if one I miss
will grow to be a mighty oak.

At six years old
Cummings said "When I grow up I want to be a poet."
"You'll starve" someone said.

don't let fear get in the way

fear is a tyrant
it forbids you from flying
taking risks
daring to write verse
speaking before an audience

it shackles your feet to a stake
lest you go in search of
the person
you want to become
and ultimately be

but you shatter those shackles
the day you realize that
you need no other
to define your life
but yourself

then you are free
to climb to the highest ledge
to journey as far as your legs will go
to write as you wish
and say what your spirit prompts

the secret to your existence
is to have no fear
which fear fears most
fearing that someday you will awake
and fearlessly be who you wanted to be

don't waste an idle thought

the fountain's water gushes upwards
mushrooms for a moment
then collapses noisily on the pond
applauding the thirty ducks
sitting on the wall
waiting for the sun to rise

don't you remember?

Peter said to his brother
it's not the same
is it

ever since Jesus left us
getting up isn't the same
the excitement's gone

i used to get up wondering
what the day would hold
where i'd go and who i'd meet

i'll never forget the day
Jesus took the hand of a girl thought dead
and told her to arise

she stood and smiled
her parents took her into their arms
as once before

i can recall that scene
as though it were
just hours ago

those were the days
no two alike
new words new dreams every day

Jesus promised that he would never leave us
he'd be at our side always
no matter where in the world we were

but it doesn't seem that he kept his promise
i don't hear his voice or see his face
he's gone and we're alone

Andrew interrupted Peter
he hasn't left us
don't you remember the last night

and what he said
as we sat around
the table

with a piece of bread in his hand
he said
   this is my body

and with a cup of wine
said
   this is my blood

then looking into our eyes
   whoever eats this bread and drinks this cup
   lives in me and i in them

he couldn't be any closer to us than that
he in us and we in him
he kept his promise

so open your eyes and ears
and see him in the faces and hear him in the voices
of those around you

from now on
my brother
no two days will be alike

walk slowly and feel the earth beneath our feet
we contemplate the moment
     and feel our feet walking
     one foot at a time
     connecting with the whole earth
at that moment
     we are on the world's stage
     and prepared to enjoy the show

we walk slowly
     take our time
     aware of where we are
     surrounded by the things
     we have known to be there always
the things pointed out to us
     by those who cared for us
     as we toddled

trees surround us
     hundreds of different kinds
     told by their trunk and leaves
look at them and wonder--

why are they not all alike
it would have been easier
     to create trees all alike
     the same shape and size

and the same with blossoms
     same color
     same shape
     same smell
     appearing on the same hillside
     at the same time of year
     with leaves dropping in the same month
     all around the world

wouldn't it have been easier
      to create all blossoms alike
      same color and smell
but the creator chose not to do that

how boring it would be
      to wake and walk each morning
      knowing that we are going to see
      the same trees and blossoms
      we have seen before
      no matter where and when we are in the world

the creator doesn't like boring us
we are grateful for that
imagine trees and blossoms made the same--and we as well
      everyone looking exactly alike
      same color
      same language

no one would bother getting up
we would have seen and heard it all before
      everyone looking alike
      talking alike
      saying the same things
      day after day
      year after year
      no conflict
      absolutely no conflict
      of mind body or soul

diversity may drive us crazy
not once in a while
      but always
but that is infinitely better than
      being bored
      every day of the week

Emmaus

two years ago
my life was scripted
i did the things
the people of Emmaus did

then Jesus came to Emmaus
his words changed my life
i can't speak for others
but they changed mine

as i listened to him
i could feel my life changing
he challenged me to rethink
the things i took for granted

everything in the world
gives praise to God
he said
if you listened you could hear the praises being sung

ordinary things like rivers
praise God falling thunderously
from high ledges
to applauding pools below

trees sing hymns
in the evening
conducted by
a western wind

stones
yes stones
sing the most mystical songs of all
called silence

after hearing him speak

i immediately became a disciple
i knew i would never be the same
and i wouldn't ever want to be

no longer did i think
that things had to be
as they always were
they could be changed

for the first time in my life
i awoke with the thought
that with him
i could make a difference

he stayed in Emmaus only for a day
then off to the towns and cities of Palestine
a small country
where word traveled fast from town to town

i followed his journey through words passed on
and went to see and hear him
whenever he was nearby
word was he was going to be in Jerusalem for the Passover

so i asked Cleopas my friend
if he wanted to walk with me to Jerusalem
and wait in the city
for Jesus' coming

we went together
but things did not turn out
as i thought
they would

the words that Jesus spoke
that changed my life

were not the words
those in charge wanted to hear

so they convicted him
of what i am not sure
and sentenced him to death
on a cross

when word spread that Jesus was dead
Cleopas said
let's go home
it has ended here

but i said no
some women say that he has risen and is alive
so let's go back by another way
we may meet him on the road

Cleopas was ready to give up
i wasn't
didn't Jesus tell us that nothing was inevitable

so let's keep seeking
keep walking
we'll find him
of that i am sure

don't you admire that disciple's spirit
for twenty-one hundred years
this unswerving companion of Cleopas
has remained nameless

don't you think it's time
to give her or him a name
how about yours
. . . . or mine

example is engraved in our hearts

words may topple mountains
split oceans
ignite fires
but free of action
are unable to move hearts

every student knows
that eloquence matters

but example matters more

when class is done
words are forgotten
deeds are not

words
are written in our pads
example
is engraved in our hearts

the whisper of kind action
is heard above the thunder of words
good teachers know that
and act accordingly

eloquent words are forgotten
kind deeds are not
like the sun moon and stars
they are remembered always

eye contact

It's all about the eyes.
Once eye contact is made
a contract has been entered.
There's no getting out of it.

The priest sees a beaten man in a ditch.
He crosses the road to avoid him.
He knows that if he doesn't
there will be no absolution.

He'll be committed to lend
the victim a helping hand
and that outreach
could go on indefinitely.

So making sure that he
doesn't catch the victim's eye
he crosses the road
and pretends
he doesn't see the bruises.

Perhaps we've done that
or something like it
when we see up ahead a man
playing a harmonica
with a straw basket by his feet
and a lonesome dollar in it
on the corner of State Street and Main.

We can lift our wrist
stare at our watch
pretend we're running behind schedule
pull out our iPhone
as though we're calling
the office to tell the manager
we'll be late.

By this time we're well past the
man with the basket at his feet
and our eyes never met.

There are very few lines in scripture
that we can identify with as readily
as we can with the priest running late
for a service at the synagogue.

the eyes of a child

According to Jesus
     sanctity isn't as hard
     to achieve
     as we are led to believe.

Give a cup of cold water
     to a child
     and we are there.

That's what he said today.
Fill a small cup
     with fresh cold water
     and hand it carefully
     to a child
     and you have it made.

Why then do we
     spend so much time
     agonizing over our mistakes
     and failings.

Just do what Jesus says.
Don't make it any harder than that.
Hand the cup carefully
     to the child
     and as you do look into her eyes
     seeing there the eyes of all children.
That's what sanctity is.

a friend of mine

Someday we'll have a chance to meet the people who
introduced us to Jesus

So today let's draw a list of authors
and their works that changed our lives

What was it they wrote
that encouraged us to become friends of Jesus

Did Cummings introduce us to Jesus' humanness
Chesterton to his common sense
and Teresa his approachability

Who inspired us
to love him personally

We know from today's reading
that Jesus did not lose his friends

They will all be there
waiting for us

We'll have an opportunity
to thank them for what they did for us

and how they inspired us to use our words
to do the same for others

and ask them did they react as we did
when Jesus introduced us to his Father
as a friend

the gardener

I look forward to early morning walks
through the garden.
They give me time to think about
the high Cs of *"Nessun dorma"*
the cathedrals of Gehry
the poems of Hopkins
the footsteps of Armstrong
the lilies of Monet.

Then when I finish thinking
I begin wondering will there ever be--
a better singer
a better architect
a better poet
a more curious explorer
a more creative artist?

Emphatically
I tell myself "Yes."

We were born
with the expectation that there
is always more to come;
someone will appear on the earth's stage
to hit a purer "C"
draw a more intriguing line
find the words to capture love's unique feeling
reach a star beyond Hubble's scope
and mix paints that finally define dawn.

We are restless creatures
and will always be so.
We were born to seek
and as long as we walk here
the questions will come
the wonderings will continue.

That's why earth is
such an exciting place to live.

And when the time comes
to end our walk here
we'll start another walk
in another garden
and we'll meet the gardener there
and say
we have so many questions
it will take forever to find their answers
and the gardener
will simply say
"I know."

golden fans

A thin sheet of ice
covers half the pond this morning.

Showing through it
is a huge oriental rug of

yellow and red leaves
designed by the wind.

Two ducks don't seem
to mind the winter's intrusion.

"As long as the fountains are spouting,
we have some paddling space."

On the shore
standing alongside Wells Street

are three gingko trees
with neat circles beneath them

filled with thousands
of tiny gold fans.

I have walked this way
many times

but never before
noticed the brilliant

difference between them
and the rusty oak leaves beside them.

It was the tick of a second
that had me turn my head today

and witness one more moment
of gratitude and awe.

greed kicks in

There is a humorous side to the
gospel story this morning.

A young man approaches Jesus
and asks what he must do
to gain eternal life.

Jesus tells him
that if he wishes eternal life
he need only keep
the commandments.

The young man
says
Which ones.

It was as though
he could pick and choose
which ones to follow.

Jesus lists six
and the young man said
that he followed all of those.
Now if he had let it go at that
he would have been
guaranteed heaven.

But no.
He wants to impress Jesus
with his zest for holiness
so he asks what else could he do
to assure a box seat in heaven.

That was a mistake.
A very big mistake.
He should have left well enough alone.

But his greed surfaced.

Now if he really wanted that seat
Jesus said
he'd have to sell all that he had
and give the proceeds to the poor.

That was too much to ask.
The young man turned
mounted his Arabian stallion
and rode off into the Judean hills.

harmony

when you find a minute
to stop and think
about the huge world around us
you shudder and shake

could things get any more
troubled than they are now
people without bread and
filled with fear

and it's been this way for
a long time
despite the hopes
we have had for this garden
that moves so easily among the stars

and it's not as though
there's no untangling
the mess we're in

the most unusual man
ever to walk with us
climbed to the top of a hill
and said--

> *climb up here with me*
> *leave yourself behind*
> *and what you seek you'll find*
> > *selflessness is the garden's harmony*

harmony heard

there is harmony in the world
    all we have to do is look
        and we will hear it

humility is conceived

We stand alone
in an open yard
on a clear dark night
and raise our eyes
to the heavens
filled with the hundred million stars.

We trust our eyes
to express our awe
at the expanse of lights
embraced in a momentary glance.

In that moment
humility is conceived
for our speck of dust
is called by God
to live beyond
the last flickers
of the heavens'
brightest stars.

hunger trumps the law

it was the Sabbath
  and the disciples were hungry
  so they picked the wheat
  from the field of Eleazar.

Eleazar confronted Jesus
  saying that his followers
  were thieves and law-breakers.

Jesus said that they were
  hungry
  and hunger trumps the law.

But it is the Sabbath
  Eleazar answered back
  and that can't be broken.

Jesus returned with
  the Sabbath was made for man
  and not the other way around
  for merciful eyes see
  a starving man
  as more sacred than the law

Even your saintly king David
  entered the Temple and out of hunger
  ate the sacred bread

The law of God is broken
  not by the hungry who eat to live
  the wheat of the earth
  but by those who
  reap it from stolen land
  and lock it behind barn doors.

an incomparable walk

five senses
are not enough
to embrace the world
at six in the morning
we need time
retentive minds
lively imaginations
an arsenal of words
and a catalog of images

so equipped
we'd be ready to walk
through the world
and appreciate its splendor

this morning
the purple beech
alongside the carousel
is approaching full leaf
we wonder
if it is aware of its colorful advent
does it feel the misty rain on its young leaves
as we do upon our faces
soft and cool

the walk today is incomparable
we have never been more aware
as we are now
of spring trees
wrinkled pond
silent rain
and the morning's soft sunrise

nor have we ever been more aware
of feeling
          hearing seeing smelling tasting yes

but feeling no
the feel of the light wind across our hands and faces
is a new awareness

all of this has been given us
to enjoy the gift of universe
how can we ever appreciate
the divine invention of the human body
and mind and spirit
they are too wonderful
to appreciate
too intricate to imagine

will there ever come a time
when we say
we have nothing more to say
but thanks

initials in the snowbank

Instead of finding the
initials ML/PK
carved into the bark of
the old Purple Beech tree
standing by the carousel,
I saw them this morning
scratched neatly
          as though with a long twig
into the deep snowbank
running up from the lily pond
to the edge of Jewell Street.

The initials on the tree
have been there for a hundred years.
These on the bank most likely
will disappear
before the week ends.
However
it doesn't mean
that the love
on the snowbank
is any less ardent
than the one commemorated
on the tree.
In fact
it conveys an urgency
on the part of ML and PK
to tell the whole world
as quickly as possible
of their undying love
--something the knife and thick bark
would not allow.

And then
as though to confirm my speculation
the full moon

who knows something about love
looked through the one big hole in the clouds
and beamed approval
just before it left for the day.

Years from now
ML and PK will walk beside the pond
look at the bank
and say
"Do you remember?"
"Yes."

That's what matters.
Not bark or snow.

Jesus came to serve

Jesus has gotten lost in the translations.
Don't ask me how that has happened.
It seems that every generation wanted Jesus
to be someone other than what he came to be: a servant.

Jesus came to be a servant.
He said so himself.
He wanted to be one of us.
No better, no worse.
Peter wanted to make him better.
I can only guess why.
Perhaps if Jesus were elevated to Messiah
Peter would rise with him.
Peter would finally get the respect
he thought he deserved
if not right away then someday down the line.
But Jesus put Peter in his place
down where he belonged
with the servants.

It was just the beginning
of refashioning Jesus.
If he were Christ the King
everyone in the court was a prince
and treated accordingly.

When was Jesus elevated from servant to king?
Time does strange things.
Perhaps his followers liked it that way,
preferring to be served rather than
to serve.

Today the times are changing.
Adjectives such as humble, sincere,
modest, and gentle are being used
when describing the one who follows the servant.

No one doubts that example is the best teacher. And the best students are those who follow the best example.

Peter tells an official
  that Jesus pays his temple tax.
The fact is
  Jesus doesn't pay taxes.
Peter is in trouble.
But to protect Peter from embarrassment
  Jesus tells him
  to go to the seashore
  bait a hook
  cast a line
  catch a fish
  open its mouth
  and there find a coin.
Then go back to the official
  hand him the coin
  saying that this
  covers the taxes of Jesus and me.

Psalm 8:

When I see the heavens
the work of your hands
the moon and stars which you arranged
what is man that you should keep him in mind
mortal man that you care for him?

Jesus is a poet

If we answered questions
on an exam
as Jesus did
when questioned by the crowd
we would not have graduated.

The crowd asked
"Do you drive out demons by Beelzebub?"
and he answered
"If I do by whom do your people drive them out?"
Question for question.

Then they asked
"Who is going to protect our possessions
if a robber stronger than our guard comes?"
Jesus answered by saying
"Whoever does not gather with me
scatters."

Then he changed the subject entirely and said
"Once a demon has been driven
from your home
don't clean it
for he'll round up seven more demons
and bring them to your tidy house."

Jesus should not be taken literally.
He did not speak in prose
as theologians do.
Nor did he ever dictate or explain what he said.

Jesus spoke in images and symbols
and left it up to the crowd
to decide what he meant:
          in other words
                    he is a poet.

Jesus wept

when Mary told Jesus
that Lazarus had died
Jesus wept

his tears came quickly
and flowed silently for memories
that would never be relived

> *where have you laid him*
> *here in this cave*
> *behind the stone*

then Jesus shouted
> *Lazarus come out*
> *untie him and set him free*

the crowd was struck dumb
Jesus went to Lazarus
and took him by the hand

together they walked
toward a clump of trees
and sat side by side on a wooden bench

Martha and Mary from a distance
watched them sit where they usually sat
when Jesus came to visit

Lazarus was the brother
Jesus didn't have
they were true friends

they'd sit on the wooden bench
and exchange
> *do you remembers*

today
Jesus told Lazarus
how much his friendship meant

it was something he failed
to say when Lazarus
was alive

now he had another chance
he wasn't going to
let it pass

Jesus said
thank you for standing by me
when others turned and walked away

Jewish storytellers

The imagination of Jewish storytellers is legendary
Danny Kaye
Mel Brooks
Henny Youngman
Jack Benny
Mae West
Carol Channing
Lucille Ball
Joan Rivers
Burns and Allen
And the list goes on
Back to the time of Moses
     and the day he led thousands of Jews out of Egypt
     into the desert in search of a land that couldn't be
          found on a map.

They wandered aimlessly for years
     until one day
     out in the middle of the desert
     with little water and tasteless manna
     Moses went missing.
He was last seen going up a mountain
     and not seen coming back down.

The Jews grew restless.
The leader who supposedly knew
     what the trip was all about
     was missing in action.
They needed him to assure them that
     God had not abandoned them.
Moses' brother Aaron had to think fast
     lest he have a rebellion on his hands.
Bring me all the gold you have
     he said.
Mind you he was talking to slaves
     who had nothing but whiplash on their backs

to show for their years of slavery.

Where they had stashed their gold
        was the question left to Jewish
        storytellers to hone
        their imaginations on for centuries.

Aaron melted down the gold and sculpted a calf
        large enough to satisfy the wanderers
        and their need for celebration.
They laughed and sang and had a merry good time
        prancing around the calf.
That is until Moses came down from the mountain top
        and raised Cain with Aaron
        then bargained with God
        to forgive the fickleness of the chosen people.
If you want to blame anyone for this idolatry
        he said to Yahweh
        blame me for abandoning your people
        and strike me from the book of life.

Yahweh said no.
You are too precious to me.
I'll keep your name in the book
        and catch up with the others later.

Since then the Jewish storytellers
        have kept audiences laughing uproariously
        hoping there would be enough tears of laughter
        to drown the tears of sorrow which came with all
        the "laters" that followed.

joy is felt not heard

the joy that comes with expectancy
explodes when they meet
at the top of the hill

Elizabeth still can't believe it
so many years of wondering why
what she wanted most and was denied
is now happening
--a child is within

what Mary had only hoped with Joseph
has happened mysteriously without him
and the joy of it
is uncontrollable
releasing a flood of poetic lines
linked to Abraham and his children
from centuries past

they collapse in each other's arms
trading joy but not understanding
for the best of joy does not allow
words construed by man
it has its own meaning
felt rather than heard

within Elizabeth its fresh touch startles the baby
something has changed
he feels it
the first to feel it
things would never be the same
and would be his
to foretell

they remain together
on the hilltop
above the sounds below

wondering
for that is all they could do
what would become
of those two to
be born of them

just enough is more than enough

The disciples panicked when they saw the crowd.
It was late and the people were hungry.
Send them away.
Have them go back to town.
They'll find food there.
We have "just enough" for ourselves.

Jesus told the disciples to sit down upon the grass
       and break their bread in two
       and learn that
       "just enough is more than enough."

the Lord said in a vision

i wish i had a vision now and then
it would make life a whole lot easier
i'd know what to do with my time
Jesus in a vision
      told Paul to go on speaking
      don't be silent
i wish Jesus would appear to me
      and tell me to keep on writing
      forget the critics
      if they think that
      you are writing too much
      about me
      too bad
keep writing
tell them that you had a vision
who is going to know
      whether or not you did
they took Paul's word for it
      didn't they
tell them that your vision
      didn't come during the night
      but in a classroom
      on a Monday afternoon
and the person who spoke to you
      didn't look anything
      like the portraits
      seen in picture books or galleries
but in fact reminded you
      of Raymond Carver
      as pictured on the back cover
      of one of his short story books
it wasn't of course
      but reminded you
      when he said
          what is it you are after
          in this life

-- then go for it

the definitions of visions
        change often
once they were nighttime things
        fuzzy and only for the holy
        but now anytime anywhere anyone

love can do it

Chances are that you wouldn't
bet on the lamb or the dove
in today's parable.

Docility and innocence
are no match
for rapaciousness and stealth.

That is
until the Spirit comes
into the story.

Love is a mighty opponent
creative
and tireless.

Provided
that is
that you call upon it.

Once engaged
there is no limit
to its plans

for outwitting
the hunger and greed
of its enemies.

Love is patient
determined
and relentless.

That's what Jesus
is saying
when he sends his disciples out.

Go into the world
bring the message I've given you
to the people.

Ignore the howling
and the hissing

and before you're done
you'll have changed
the face of the world.

loving one another

It's five o'clock in the afternoon.
I'm home sitting on the fourth floor balcony
overlooking Gold Street.

There is a bus stop
beneath my balcony
and an Indian woman and a little girl
holding her hand
are just getting off the bus.

Time stands still.
For years women
have been getting off buses
holding children's hands
and walking up streets like Gold Street
somewhere in the world.

Things change
but what matters stays the same:
a woman and a child
getting off a bus
holding hands
loving one another together.

mayflies

It's five-thirty in the afternoon
and I am on the balcony
thinking about mayflies.
They live at most for twenty-four hours
eating, propagating, and
picking on us.

Take my word for it.
When I walk through Bushnell Park
at six-thirty on a hot May morning
the mayflies are all over me
in my eyes ears and nose.
They drive me crazy.

If that's the case
why do I walk through the park in May?
Because it's spring.
And walking through the park in spring
is a parental thing to do.
I get a chance
to watch the birth of trees
flowers and grass.

And being the proud parent
of a family like this
in my neighborhood of creation
is reason enough to put up with the mayflies.

And besides what else do I have to think about
sitting on my balcony
at five-thirty on a summer afternoon?

Oh, I suppose I could think about
what Ramsey thinks about
as he walks with me through the park each morning.
He never says a word.

He just looks and barks at strange little dogs
and sniffs every single thing that is sniffable--
fallen branches
chicken bones
empty Subway bags
and dropped donuts.
Oh and he barks at the twenty ducks
sitting on the wall of the pond.

For all I know
he is thinking about his genealogy
and how he ended up here with me
having to get up early
on cold winter mornings
trudge through the snow
freeze his paws
eat dry biscuits for breakfast
and take a nap.

Ah, the mystery of life!!
To awake and begin again
not having the slightest idea of what is ahead.
Isn't that the greatest gamble
of all?

miracles are unimaginable

The disciples stood with Jesus by a Mulberry tree
when they asked Him
to increase their faith.

"Increase!" Jesus said "You have more than enough faith
to say to this tree uproot yourself
and be planted in the sea."

Bartholomew
a disciple who rarely spoke
said
"That's unimaginable."

Jesus responded
"Miracles always are."

morning prayer

"As the cataract of ignorance falls
from off the eyesight of my soul,
 I realize that all this huge Creation
round about me is the Word."   *Ku Sang*

Both fountains are gushing.
There are twenty-eight ducks on the pond.
And there are ten schools of tiny goldfish in it.
I don't see any Koi.
The heron isn't here this morning.
The Hog River is flowing fast through the play area.
Four of the eight bullfrogs are spouting.
Eleven tortoises are headless.
A girl wrote on the side of the chute-the-chute that she
          needs a boyfriend.
Paul is sleeping on the bench by the Perry sculpture.
Dorothy on her way to her job at the shelter has yet to be
          seen.
Crows are trying to sing.
Athletes in shorts are running to stay in shape.
Five dogs are busy sniffing trees and lampposts.
Ramsey's rolling on his back every chance he gets.
When he isn't rolling he is looking for his friend Smokey.
The sun is hidden.
I can't catch a slice of the blue moon.
I miss the felled ancient maple tree.

Fundamental to the teaching of Jesus is vigilance.
Nothing is ordinary.
It changes moment by moment
and if you're not awake
you miss the daily revelations of the Word all around you.

a new script

At the first stop on his journey
Jesus wrote a script
that the Pharisees
had yet to read.

To shield the bridal couple from shame
Jesus gave them enough wine
to keep their friends
singing and dancing for days.

And he followed the same script
when he sat around the table with
his friends at the home of Martha and Mary
in the quiet suburb of Bethany
or in the homes of the rich and powerful
in noisy Jerusalem
or on the peaceful hillside overlooking
the Sea of Galilee
after a successful day of fishing.

Jesus wasn't saying that
his cousin John was wrong
telling his followers to fast always
but times and people change
as does the definition of holiness.
And new wine cannot be put into
        old wine skins
lest they split and the new goes down the drain
to join the sour.

no bill of goods

After hearing what Jesus
      had to say about becoming
      a disciple
      anyone thinking about it
      had better think twice
      before making
      any commitment.

Jesus tells the crowd
      that the path disciples will have to walk
      isn't easy--
      they'll have to be as shrewd as serpents
      to avoid wolves.

That would have been enough to discourage me.
I had no idea what
      being as "shrewd as serpents" meant.
I didn't even like looking at snakes
      slithering along hiking paths
      or sticking their heads out of the pond
      just when I was about to stick my toe in
      to test the temperature
      never mind imitating their shrewdness.

And then there was all that about being scourged publicly
      in a synagogue
      or having your own children turn you in for
          execution.
      That was too much.

Jesus did not paint a pretty picture
      of discipleship.
He made it as grim as he could
      so that no follower
      could ever say that he or she was
      sold a bill of goods.

overlooking Gold Street

From my balcony overlooking
Gold Street
I am watching people get off the five o'clock bus
and head up toward Main Street.

An old man with a limp and baggy pants just stepped off.
On his head is a small green cone.
It looks like a pistachio ice cream cone
turned upside down.
A duffle bag hangs off his shoulder.
Alone on the sidewalk
he walks in circles
small circles
and goes nowhere.
He's bewildered.
There's no one to talk to.
The bus pulls away from the curb
and heads up the street.
Without looking one way or the other
he steps off the curb into the street
and limps toward the other side.
Horns blow and brakes jam to a stop.
He keeps going.
Once across the street he finds
      what he didn't expect to find--
a field of stones
      huge stones.
He goes to a brown boulder close to the sidewalk
and puts his hand on it and keeps it there.
I wonder what he's doing.
He's motionless
with his hand resting on the stone.
A gentleman coming down the street stops
looks at the green cone on the man's head
and smiles.

From my balcony I watched
this dramatic performance
of today's gospel.
The shepherd goes in search of the reckless lamb
and finds him.
The woman goes in search of the precious coin
and finds it.
The father goes in search of his misguided son
and finds him.
The essence of all the parables Jesus came to teach is
wrapped in this one:

      He came in search of those lost
      and rejoices when they are found.

overnight revolution

This morning
a calf and a lion walk hand in hand
down by the riverside
a wolf relaxes at a lamb's house party
and a child plays Monopoly in a cobra's backyard.
Yesterday they were diners and dinners.
Today they are bosom buddies.
There must have been an overnight revolution.
And peace won.

the paradox

Whoever finds his life
       will lose it--
whoever loses his life
       will find it .

That's a sentence
standing on its head
to attract attention.

So let us attend to it.

If morning comes
accompanied with the thought
that finally you have gotten your life
under control and it is time
to sit back and rest easy,
       you will know that you have lost it.
For life by definition is what is ahead of you.
And the desire to reach it is unrelenting.

Discontentment is the prod
to leave the life which isn't you
and seek the one which is.

And you will know that you have found it--
       for joy accompanies the discovery.

And you'll sense
       when you are getting close.
The excitement builds.
Your life is within reach.
Joy is about to explode.

Finally
       your hands wrap around it--
       your life is in your hands.

But no sooner is it there
          than restlessness moves in--
                    the surest sign that you have found it
                    writing the ultimate paradox--
                              discontentment is the offspring of joy.

the park changes daily

Ordinary things need watching.
They change daily.
Nothing remains the same.
Everything changes.

Oak trees fall.
Skylines switch.
Rivers run.
Horses prance.
Blossoms vanish.
Ducklings swim.

Early morning is the best time to attend to ordinary things.
It is then that they speak to you.
They have your undivided attention.
For the morning is quiet.

pink carpets

we are well into May now
and the cherry trees are
dropping their petals
on the pond

floating on the surface
of the pond
woven by the wind
they stay together

like small pink rugs
randomly placed
on the living room floor
of the park

i wonder if the heron
standing tall on the rim of the drain
appreciates
the rug at its feet

poetry and prose

why is it that i
can sit in a room
and hear words differently

poetry and prose
are as different
as sunrise is from sunset

it is not endings
that matter as much
as what preceded the end

the heavens declare
    the glory of God
it is not enough
    that the heavens
declare the magnificence of God
    they announce it
proclaim it
    publish it
assert it
    broadcast it
it is as though
    the heavens
cannot be silenced
    they keep on
shouting for all to hear
    the glory of God
for those with
    ears to hear
the dome
    is a concert hall
filled with
    classical music
with concertos
    attending to
every star
    every planet
every constellation
    every new array
every sun's rising
    every moon's setting
it is one thing to hear the music
it is quite another
    to put it into words

Ramsey's nap

When Rams falls asleep in the afternoon
by my chair in the den
he has a big smile on his face.
The "old geezer" has fallen asleep in his chair
he says to himself
and I can have an uninterrupted nap for myself!
Heaven!
Heaven on earth.
What a joy.
No bothering me about taking a walk.
None of that.
A nap.
Time to sleep and think about
the snack I'll have when he wakes up
whenever that will be.
But he's a good "old geezer."
He feeds me
takes me for a walk
introduces me to his friends
serves me breakfast lunch and supper
takes me for another walk
pats me on the head at bedtime
regulates the temperature in the room
          summer and winter
and says "good night"
as though he thinks I don't know what he is talking about.
But I do know what goes through his head.
After all we dogs were here for thousands of years
before his kind ever set foot on this planet.

reach defines us

since we were born
with the wish
to fulfill all of our dreams
we'll probably fall short of satisfaction

we'll most likely never hit high C
or end a line of poetry with the word
which ties the whole poem together perfectly
or scale the highest mountain before we're fifty
or preach a homily with the insight
into the life of Jesus which has escaped
mystics and theologians for the past
twenty centuries

no
fulfilling all of our dreams
is a goal that is always a yard ahead
of our reach

but that shouldn't stop us from reaching
it's the reach that defines us
it is the cross of the disciple
for when we think we have given everything
and there's no more reach in us
we discover who we are
our hand closes around the goal
and that's the ultimate satisfaction

red-yellow

It's autumn and the leaves
on the Linden trees across the street
are changing from green to red-yellow
and I wonder if the trees notice the difference.

At six-thirty this morning
the moon
is but a sliver of its former self
and I wonder if its pride is hurt.

Yesterday there were thirteen ducks
paddling on the pond
swept clean of paper cups and shopping bags
and I wonder if they appreciate it.

sat on the shore of the sea

Jesus went out of the house and sat on the shore of the sea.
That's the opening sentence of today's story about Jesus.
I like it.
A simple sentence.
Right to the point.
Jesus went out of the house and sat on the shore of the sea.

Alone and quiet was his usual morning habit.
The difference today was the sea.
The rhythm of the waves and sound of the wind
      revived memories of those
      who called his name from roadsides
      or followed him from town to town
      or listened as he taught in the synagogues.

His mind went from one memory to another.
Voices and faces came to him from everywhere.
His eyes and ears couldn't keep up with them.
That is until the vivid memory of a wheat field appeared.
Then the rapid flow of his memories stopped.
He focused on a wheat field
      that he and his friends had walked through just a
         few weeks ago.

He remembered
      how the wheat shafts bent in the wind
      and how the smell of the ripening wheat pleased
         him.

Now sitting by the shore
      quiet and alone
      his mind focused on something which it had missed
         before--
      the day will come
      he thought
      when that walk through the field with his friends

will mean much more to them
than it did that day weeks ago.

That day came sooner than he thought it would
While sitting at table with his friends
  he took in his hands
  a piece of bread
  broke it
  saying
  this which the earth has given
  is my body for the life of the world.
  Take and eat.
  Do this in *memory* of me.

the secret of happiness

What is the secret of happiness
the student asked the sage.

The sage responded
stretch out your hand and
reach what you can.

The student reacted immediately.
Oh no.
That's too easy.
It must be much harder than that.

The sage paused
trying to gauge the young student's will
then said
Yes.
You are right.
It is more difficult than that.
The secret of happiness is to
stretch out your hand to reach what you cannot.

The student stood still for a moment
thought of what was said
then said
I will.
Thank you.
We will meet again.

Then he set out in search of happiness.
Years passed.
He traveled the world
met the rich and the poor
read all the books he could get his hands on
learned to play the mandolin
tended to the sick
sat quietly daily and enjoyed the silence.

He was always thinking
always stretching
always reaching for things beyond his grasp.
Things like--
erasing the word "mine" from all dictionaries
writing an anthem that rendered "hate" irrational
giving every child a breakfast menu
then filling their orders.

Reaching for these things and many others
while beyond his grasp
was his happiness.

Years passed and at times
his arms grew tired
but he stretched and reached
until one day
he felt his hand grasp
the hand of another
and with its holding
heard a familiar voice say
come follow me.
He did and was led to a banquet hall full to overflowing.
Amazing
he said out loud.
Yes.
A*mazing*
but know that
despite the enormous crowd
there is always room
at the table of the King
for those who
stretch and reach
for that which they cannot grasp.

sell what you have

a rich man ran up to Jesus
and asked for
a guarantee to heaven

obey the commandments
sell what you have
and follow me

the man
turned around
and walked away

Jesus said
that it is easier for a camel
to squeeze through a needle's eye

than for
the rich
to make it through

does that mean that those
who aren't rich
make it through easily

no
for prejudice is often a treasure
heavier than a bag of gold

so before anyone thinks
that they've made it because
their bank account is meager

they must
sell their vices
the ones that trouble them the most

then the eyelet becomes an arch
and their camels
can canter through

she trusted Jesus

a sinful woman
walked into Simon's party
the guests knew her by reputation
she didn't care
what mattered was Jesus
and she wanted to be as close to him as she could be
for he was the man
that people said
was the most unusual man
they had ever met

she saw him across the courtyard
and weaved her way through the crowd
reached his table
and without a word
knelt by his side

the guests went silent
people watched her tears
fall on the feet of Jesus
bathing them
then with her undone hair
she dried them

after that nothing mattered
not the silence
not the stares
the risk had been taken
she trusted Jesus
she trusted Him
with all the moments of her life
and their whys
forgiveness was immediate
her trust demanded it
and her heart felt it
with a flush of new life

sing a new song

When God first saw us
we weren't very much to look at.
We could barely stand up straight
couldn't speak
and had no idea what
a pen and paper were.
Yet
God went so far as to say
that we were good to keep.
God knew that someday
we would find ways to say
what was on our mind
and not much later than that
how to put those sounds
into color.
Once that happened
an inspired one among us
would write Psalm 96 telling
the heavens to be glad
the earth to rejoice
the sea to resound
the plains to dance with joy
and the forests' trees
to wave their hands in celebration
all in gratitude for creation.

It's a long time
since Psalm 96 was written
but its admonition
is current:
sing a grateful song today:
                    --what will our song be?

sing like a nightingale

If you have ever had a chance
to hear a murder of crows
witness the capital punishment of
a fellow crow who had
betrayed them
you'll understand why crows should
never dare criticize
the singing of finches or any other birds
for that matter.

Their cawing at such an event is horrendous loud
         unrelenting,
and nerve-wracking.
It's no wonder that folklorists years ago
referred to a flock of crows as a "murder."
I heard one of their performances
not long ago
coming from the elm trees
near the park and it was murderous.

I recalled that episode easily
after reading this morning's gospel
and resolved never to criticize
the performance of any other bird
until I could sing like a nightingale.

sit still with scripture

Sit still with scripture.
Sit still in stillness.
Sit in a comfortable chair away from noise.
It is you and the divine words.
Concentrate on their sound.
Imagine them being spoken.
Feel them being spoken.
Hear them being spoken.
Imagine the rhythm of the words working together.
Let them sink into your mind.
Remember them.
Memorize them.
Carry them with you through the day.
Make them your own.
Reflect on how they affect your life.
Live them through the day.
Carry them with you wherever you go.
Bring them with you to eternity
for it is there that they will be understood.

the smug ones

Jesus said to Matthew
    follow me.
Matthew said to Jesus
    follow me.

Jesus followed Matthew
    to his home
    and once the word got out
    that the holy one from Nazareth was there
    the place filled quickly.

In those days
    if you left the gate to the courtyard open
    passers-by felt free to come in
    to nibble on *hors d'oeuvres*
    and sip wine and sit where they wished.
    Many sat next to Jesus
    especially tax collectors and sinners.

The smug ones stood on the edge of the yard
    kibitzing about the motley group that came
    tax collectors and sinners
    and how could Jesus
    who was reputed to be so holy
    tolerate the closeness of people like that.

A smug one speaks just loud enough to be heard
    covers his mouth with the back of his hand
    to feign discretion but not enough to stifle
        everything.

Jesus heard them and said
    if everyone were saintly
    there would have been no reason
        for me to have come
    so be kind enough to put name tags

on the sinners
so I don't waste my time
talking to the holy ones.

space for the spirit

i don't mind cooking
in fact i enjoy it
i ask
what beats cooking linguine
with shrimp and lemon sauce
served with an
Italian Caesar salad made with sun dried tomatoes
and anchovies

i don't mind the cooking
it's waking up in the morning
and seeing the mess of dishes
waiting for me in the kitchen
it's the cleaning up
i don't like

but one thing is sure
if i like cooking
i have to make room
for the next set of pots and pans
and of course
all the good things
--see above--
that go into the recipe
so get rid of the mess

if i want the Spirit to come into my life
i have to make room for her
by getting rid of the
pots pans and dirty dishes
which are other words for
ego
pride
jealousy
and all of the dirty vices
that clutter up the counter

i've heard that the Spirit likes
a big salad
followed by
shrimp with lemon sauce
over linguine
so if i'm going to invite her
i had better clean up the mess
in the kitchen

Tabitha–another chance

a busy morning
Rams and i were
in the park by six-thirty
our usual time

as we walk
side by side
he attends to the things
that interest him
and i to those that interest me

i noticed the mallard was still alone
his mate is somewhere
sitting on the eggs

the goldfish have hatched
hundreds of them
were gathered in the shallows
at the north end of the pond

surprisingly
the heron wasn't here
poised for fishing

and i couldn't see
the mammoth koi fish
i have no idea where they're hiding

i saw my old friend Andrew
on his way to work at six forty-five
and he told me
that the koi fish here in the lily pond
are like minnows
compared to the ones in Elizabeth Park

the fountains here haven't been turned on yet

the children's play area has been swept clear of leaves
the tortoises are still headless
the frogs aren't spouting
and the Hog River is dry

but the cherry trees along Jewell Street
have blossomed
the crocuses are up
and the grass is turning green

so it has been another busy morning
different from yesterday as usual
and that's the way
the Spirit wants it to be
don't you think that Tabitha
looked at the ordinary things of life differently
when she was given another chance

teach me to paint

He was sitting alone
    by a lily pond
    with his brushes paints and easel
    when i interrupted him.

Please excuse me
    monsieur Monet
    but do you have a minute to teach
    me how to paint.

Surely.
I would be happy to.
Take your palette
    and daub it with red blue green and yellow paints.
Hold your brush just so.
Stare at the multicolored lilies in the pond
    and listen
    they will tell you what to do.

Monsieur you must be kidding.
It can't be that easy
    to paint as wonderfully as you
    just by staring and listening
    to what flowers
    have to say.

Yes it is.
Take my word for it
    look and listen
    and soon you will discover
    how to mix your paints
    and allow your brush
    to follow the rhythm
    of the lilies as they dance
    upon the pond.

Be persistent
and before you know it
you'll be painting masterpieces
fit to be hung
on gallery walls.

teach us to pray

Teach us to pray his disciples said
Jesus ignored the reference to John
I'll teach you how to pray
Be still and be aware that you are talking to the Father
So say Our Father
Not my Father or the Father of a few
But Father of all
All in every corner of the world
Of every shape and size
Every color and tongue

Thy kingdom come
Not by imposition
Not by arms
But by our will matching yours

Give us bread
Not for some but for all
Every day and everywhere

And forgive us our sins
As we forgive those who have stepped on us
Not by evening the score
But by liberating us from any memory of the past

And once free of all that binds us
Lead us away from anything
Which might tempt us to do otherwise

And keep in mind
As you say these words
That words are seeds if clenched die
But cast the garden grows

Thank you. You are welcome.

The Pharisee went to the temple to pray.
He stood in the center courtyard
looked up and told God:
"I am not like the rest of men
greedy smug dishonest stingy unfaithful
gluttonous and lazy.
I'm a good man
unlike the one standing over there.
If he and others were as good as I Lord
you'd have a wonderful world."

But the Pharisee's words fell on deaf ears.
The Lord doesn't listen to monologues of conceit.
He listens only to soundless words of gratitude.

When you pray then
be grateful for your original life
and the amazing creation around you.

Be grateful for the thoughts that fill your mind
and feelings that stir your emotions.
They are uniquely yours
and are meant to delight challenge and inspire you
to live fully the singular life you have been given.
Make notes of your daily thoughts and feelings
for they are your only map to self-discovery and
          contentment.
Remember your life is one of a kind
and if you don't live it
it will never be lived.

And be grateful for the amazing creation that surrounds
          you.
Walk as a guest on this planet not as a visitor.
Look up to see Mars escape the claws of Leo
          on an October dawn

and listen to the falling water of a nearby fountain.
Applaud its brilliant performance.
On a morning like this
your soul will say grace
before you've had a chance to speak.
If you walk slowly and pause often
you'll be surprised by the innumerable gifts
creation invites you to open.
Open them
        or they will forever remain wrapped.

The finest prayer to God is "Thank you."
And the best way to say it is by living your life
        as fully as you can.
And when the time comes to meet The Lord face to face
you can present him with a gift he had never received
        before
your unprecedented life brought to its fullness
one of a kind in all of time.
Won't God be surprised?
And to you he'll say "Thank you."
And you'll respond graciously "You are welcome."

there will be more than enough

At the sound of Mary's voice
John leapt in Elizabeth's womb
knowing that the Messiah had come.

Years later
John saw Jesus coming toward him
through the tall grass along the Jordan River
and said aloud--

*Behold the Lamb of God
        who takes away the sins of the world.*

Jesus recalls these memories
when he hears that John has died.
He is shocked by the news and wants to be alone.
He asks Peter to pull in his boat
to take him to the far side of the sea.

But the people following Jesus
will not let him leave their sight.
They walk as fast as they can
along the shore of the sea
hoping to keep ahead of the boat.
Jesus can see them
the young and old
the feeble and strong.

As the boat lands
part of the crowd is already there.
Jesus asks himself
*Do I stay here with them
or move to a quiet place?
I have lost John
the cousin I loved.*

But no sooner does he step ashore

see their faces
and hear their voices
his decision is made.

It is late
a disciple says.
Send them home.
They are hungry.

No.
Have them sit.
We will feed them.

But we have here
only five loaves and two fish.

We will feed them.
Have them sit on the hillside.

He then blesses the bread and fish
and says to his disciples
share these with those who are here
and there will be enough.

Are you sure?

Yes, there will be enough
. . . . more than enough.

to live attentively

it is not about conclusions
it is about beginnings

it is not about grabbing
it is about reaching

it is not about satisfaction
it is about expectation

it is not about yesterdays
it is about tomorrows

it is not about achievements
it is about dreams

it is not about rest
it is about restlessness

it is not about fullness
it is about running over

the secret is
to live attentively

to live simply
to live well

only to discover
that we have only just begun

and that is
what it is all about

transfiguration

The morning started simply enough.
Jesus turned to his friends
Peter James and John
and said
"Come with me to the top of the mountain."
Why just we?
There are others.
And why a mountain?
If just to talk
why not a grove of trees
or a restful waterside?
Why a steep climb
up a mountainside?
But their questions didn't stop them.
They followed as they promised they would.

At the top of the mountain
extraordinary things began to happen
things they had never seen or heard before.
The face of Jesus started to shine
      as brightly as the sun
his brown robe became an eye-blinding white
the prophets Moses and Elijah appeared from nowhere
and from a cloud huge enough
      to cover the mountaintop
came a voice saying
      "This is my beloved son
      with whom I am well pleased."
Peter James and John
were terrified by all of this
and fell to the ground motionless
until Jesus rested his hand upon their shoulders saying
      "Rise up, and do not be afraid."

Could it have been
that Peter James and John

didn't know
didn't have the slightest idea
who this traveling man from Nazareth was
this man who could feed thousands
of hungry people on a hillside
with a handful of bread and fish
fill glasses of wine for the
family and friends of newlyweds
or tell ten lepers to dance
all the way to the temple courtyard.

Finally they blurted out
>*"You are the Messiah*
>*the foretold of the prophets--*
>*the Son of God.*
>*For three years*
>*we have walked by your side*
>*and didn't know who you were.*
>*How could we have been so blind?"*

How could we be so blind?

trash barrel

There's a trash barrel
at the exit from the park
onto Wells Street.

Into it I throw the empty beer and soda cans
that I've picked up
on my walk.

What else should I throw
into the barrel?

Irreversible regrets,
vain hopes,
and sour angers.

All these should go into the barrel.
No need to carry them any longer.
They are trash.

The park is beautiful
when the trash is thrown away.
So is life.
Get rid of the trash.

tropical breeze

Rams and I met Mike
sitting on a bench next to Elm Street
at 6:05 this morning.
He had come from the Park Street shelter.
He was smoking a cigarette
          and coughing.
He wanted to pet Rams.
I gave Mike a biscuit to give him.
"He loves me" Mike said.
"How old is he?"
"About thirteen." I said.
He continued to rub Ramsey's head and back
saying
"He loves me."

****

Rams and I continued
our walk through the park.
There was a tropical breeze blowing through it.
Sixty-six degrees!
I was wearing a light jacket.
Quite different from the layers
of sweaters
heavy sweat pants
wool hat and gloves
that I had been wearing
the last two weeks.
We walked slowly
looking at the landscaping
in front of the renovated perfect six brownstone house
on the corner of Elm and Clinton--
          well done.

*****

We crossed Elm joined Trinity
and then down to Jewell to the pond
and the walkway around it.
Our walk around the pond
        is standard.
We always check out
the Harmony sculpture
and the two fountains.
The breeze blew a light spray of fountain water
over us and wrinkled the surface of the pond.
We walked slowly
and watched fallen leaves race
to see which ones would get into the pond first.
They were enjoying the competition.
I didn't see any ducks.
But I did hear the acorn shells crunching beneath my feet.
Fallen leaves
crunching shells--
        Autumn is ending.

******

Back home and Rams is on his bed.
He's got his "toy doll" with him.
This is something new.
It's the first one he hasn't shredded.
Others he's torn apart in a week.
This one he has had since last Christmas.
Now it's next to his muzzle and under his left paw.
Why? All of a sudden. A bed mate.
If I'm ever tempted to think that
I know what's going on
        in his head,
someone ought to take my pen away.

twin oriental oaks

A few years ago
did we worry about
a dying tree?

No. Now we do.
One of the twin oaks
in the park is dying slowly.

The trunk is rotting
and its scrawny limbs
are ready to drop.

It's about to die
and its twin knows it.
They've been together since birth.

Who will it talk to
when its brother is gone?
The spruce nearby?

Rams and I doubt it.
The spruce was born here
and never learned Chinese.

The twins came from China.
They grew up there
and often gossiped about the old days.

Soon nothing.
One gone
the other left alone.

People cry
when they lose
the one they love.

Will the oak cry
when it awakes
and sees its twin gone?

Will Ramsey notice
if it's crying?
I bet he will.

He won't see tears
but surely he'll sense its sadness
and say he's sorry.

ugly pine tree

It's close to four o'clock.
I'm on the patio at Shorty's place.
It's been a delightful day
clear skies temperature in the sixties
and cardinals singing their special songs
I'm studying the tall ugly pine tree
which stands down at the edge of the marsh.
This isn't something new.
I've been doing this twice a year for the past fifteen years.
Shorty let's me use her place
to look at the marsh study the pine tree
think read and write.

Over these years
the pine tree has gotten uglier.
Poison ivy has climbed two thirds of the way up its trunk
aged branches have been broken by the wind
and one bare limb looks like
a heron anxious to leave on a moment's notice.

But despite the mistreatment of time
there is a majesty about the tree.
It stands as straight as it can
looking out over the brown and green grasses of the marsh
to the soft rolling mountains in the east
and at Matthew's Pond peeking through them.
This whole scene is its kingdom.
It is in charge of the marsh
and the billowing willow tree and slender oak
on either side of it
gladly assign it this duty.

Each year when I come to study the tree
I concentrate on the beauty of its ugliness.
It seems sublimely content with being just what it is--

sovereign of Bass River Marsh--
and that contentment makes it beautiful.
Pretension alone renders one ugly.

we alone have walked our path

no one knows us but ourselves
for we alone have walked our path
one footstep at a time
attentively
we have time now to retrace the steps
and in retracing discover who we have become
far different from who we'd thought we'd be
when we stepped first upon the path
the discovery need not be for publication
it is ours alone and appreciated in our silence
we fear the day
when someone will attempt to define
who we were
without knowing the path we walked

we are chosen

imagine Jesus in
      Cana or Jerusalem or Bethany
      or anywhere
the blind scream his name as he walks by
the crippled interrupt him as he teaches in the synagogue
lepers pull at his cloak wanting to be cleansed

what patience he had
what concentration
he could do it easily we say
      for he was chosen

well so are we
we have all been chosen
      by poured water and the spirit

if we let Jesus live in us
      we can do the things he did
      attend to what people say
      look them in the eye when they speak
      call them by name
      and incorporate them into our lives

impossible
Jesus is asking us to do the impossible

yes he is
every morning in prayer
      he asks
      and we hear him if we stay silent

we can hear Jesus ask us
      to give the best to every thing we do
      to every word we write
      to every word we speak
      to respond to those who call

        to those who interrupt
        to those who don't wear cologne

we are not ordinary people
we are extraordinary
not better
        but more aware
which is the heart of humility
we learned that from Jesus

we live as we love

Our life
       is our life's thoughts
              lived
If we live
      as hired
            we do what we must
If we live
      as we love
            there is no price
To wake satisfied
      is an ending
            otherwise a beginning

we miss so much

Today when Jesus sat in the synagogue
        and taught from the scriptures
        we were startled.

We grew up with him
        and thought we knew
        everything there was to know about him--
        an ordinary man
        a hard worker
        and a neighbor easy to be with.

Then at thirty
        he left us
        without saying where he was going
        or what he was going to do.

We never expected he'd come back to us
        as a teacher
        prepared to explain the scriptures
        as simply and
        as powerfully as he did today
        or do the things
        people say he's done in other towns--
        sights to the blind
        sounds to the deaf
        and in nearby Cana
        wine to empty glasses.

Could it be that he is telling us
        we miss so much
        when we define things and people
        as ordinary?

what is it i want

when i got to the Bay this morning
a slight wind was ruffling the water
and the small waves reaching the shore
could barely be heard
this year there's a huge hard rubber tube
stretching far out into the sea
sucking in sand to deposit
on the shrinking South Yarmouth shore

i was alone and wondering
about my life
now that i am eighty
will I have the health to be able
        to keep walking
        to take care of myself
        to live on my own

friends with whom to share ideas
ideas about the lives we've lived
and whether or not those lives mattered

or at least one person
who needs you because
she loves you and is happy she does

or at eighty is it all about desire
the desire to keep thinking
and trying to say
something that has yet to be said
and if said matters

it is not only good health
there has got to be
curiosity passion contentment

something has to be there

or you go on breathing
and taking up space

waiting to die
without making much of a fuss
and hoping that the end
is all that you hoped that it would be
the first step
of a new beginning

the life that was started here
and lived fully because
we believed that

it was only the start
of a story
that will never end

who can count

who can count the grains of sand
that ring our many seas
or the drops of rain
that fall from cloudy skies
or number the days of eternity
                    no one can

who can set a foot upon the moon
or see the ocean's floor
or exceed the speed of sound
no one can
or so we thought
                    not too long ago

but when we did
what we thought could not be done
we surpassed the limits put on mind and imagination
and creation's story
                    flipped another page

what is this compared to faith
when all is possible
to those who believe
devils leave
and those who seemed dead arise
                    help my unbelief

who's to blame

after hearing this parable again
i'm confused
whom do i blame for the failure
      the seed for not flourishing as hoped
      or the sower for poor aim

could i reasonably expect
a seed tossed among a thicket of thorns
to flourish unless it were a thistle seed

or expect a seed thrown on a pathway
to grow as anything but
a weed

or one cast upon rocks
to be something other than moss
clinging to a huge rock

the sower
      read preacher
rather than telling the community
who they are supposed to be
thereby missing the point
should invite them to discover for themselves
who they are
and what they are to make of their lives

there is a place in the world
for splendid roses
but a place too
for moss thistles and weeds
which surprise us by their beauty
when we least expect them to

i think that's what Jesus means by this parable
if so my confusion is hereafter put to rest

why are you looking up

Jesus took his disciples to Bethany
a small town two miles outside of Jerusalem
They had been there before many times
Martha and Mary friends of Jesus lived there
It was there that Jesus told his disciples
that he was going to the Father

So the disciples raised their eyes heavenward
thinking that this is where the Father was

But Jesus had something else in mind
The Father is everywhere
So don't look up
You are looking in the wrong place
He tells them to go back to Jerusalem
The Father is there
with the artisans shopkeepers teachers
Wherever people are God is there
So if you wish to find me
don't spend your time
looking to the skies
I am at the Father's side
Look to the people standing by you
Yes
Turn and look at those around you
I am there

why fishermen

Jesus chose fishermen to be his disciples
      because they were workmen
Used to the ups and downs of ordinary life
Some days the sea was as calm as a mirror
Other days as uproarious as a landslide
Some days the Sea of Galilee was packed with fish
Others days as empty as a tipped bucket
Fishermen had to deal with what the day brought
Get up
Cast the nets
Pull in the nets
Clean the nets
Bring the fish to market and get a good price
Bring the fish to market and get a pittance
They had flexible temperaments
They would take in stride the unbendable opinions
      of the scribes
      and prejudices of the priests
That's the temperament Jesus was looking for
He found it in fishermen
They stayed with him
      and turned out to be
      all he thought they would be

why you came

The gospel we just heard
Tells us that
Simeon woke up every day
Thinking
Today may be the day
That I meet The Lord
I had better be prepared for the meeting

When the young girl
Put the baby into his arms
Simeon didn't shudder or shake
There were no trumpet blasts
No songs from the heavens
Just an unusual feeling
Simeon knew that he had met the Lord
He felt it
His dream had been fulfilled
Things would never be the same
Not himself
    not the world
        not anyone in the world
Nothing would ever be the same

At that moment
He gave up his fear of dying
And began the relentless pursuit of
Discovering the reasons why he came

And that's what Simeon is telling us
With each waking
Be prepared
He says
To meet the Lord
In unexpected places
And at the oddest times
There won't be any shakes or shudders

No trumpet blasts
No songs from heaven
Just an unprecedented feeling
That you had met The Lord
By a hospital bed
On the pages of a book
In the words of a friend
And at that meeting
Everything changed
You would never be the same
You'd awake each day prepared
To pursue relentlessly why you came
Into this world . . . .
        which is life's definition
        not death's

wisdom

walking barefoot on a lonely beach
i kicked free from the sand a jewel
it appeared to be a pearl

the jeweler said it was
probably a pearl broken loose
from a necklace

i took it home
and put it on a glass table
by my chair

along with a piece of zircon crystal
a bowl of pistachios
and Labrador bookends

i am going to keep it there
to remind me of wisdom
that appears unexpectedly

ignored often when in a hurry
but treasured
when attended to carefully

now on the glass table
it joins other pieces of wisdom
scattered around my room

that appeared unexpectedly
through the years
and in the strangest places

but like scrambled letters of the alphabet
when put together properly
tell a lifetime story

words get in the way

A father asks a miracle of Jesus
  My daughter has died.
  Will you give her back her life?
Jesus turns to follow the father
  to his home.
On the way
  a woman sees Jesus
  sneaks up behind him
  and touches--
  only touches--
  the tassel of his robe.
Jesus turns and without a word
  cures her.
It was her faith that did it
  not words.
While sitting here in chapel
  praying is presence.
We don't need words.
  Sometimes
  in fact
  they get in the way
  and we end up talking to ourselves.

wrinkled sheets

Monday:
Dawn has wrapped a broad red band
around the horizon.

Tuesday:
Dawn has replaced the red band with
a massive range of dark clouds
pretending to be mountains.
And above it there's an orange glow
outlining fake tree tops and rolling hills.

The pictures in the gallery
of creation change daily.
Each morning there's something different.

Wednesday:
Today it's the waves which entertain me.
How to describe them?
They remind me of wrinkled satin sheets
thrown casually across a double bed.
Tomorrow I may find them pressed.

Thursday:
No, I didn't find them pressed.
They are tumbling wildly
attacking the sandy beach
repeatedly
then heading back out
to prepare another charge,
this time perhaps the boulders in the jetty.

Friday:
Pouring rain and wind
baffling the sea gulls.
Dawn must lie awake all night

writing the script of the next show
to appear on stage as soon as
the curtain rises.

you'll know

When the blue heron
        spreads its wings wide
        and glides smoothly to its
        pedestal in the lily pond
        when the fountain's falling waters
        applaud the robin's song
        when dogwood trees bloom to
        preach the message of redemption
        then you will know
        that summer is near.

Today from the crowd of people
        who came to hear him speak
        Jesus chose seventy-two of them
        to go to the towns of Israel
        ahead of him
        preaching that the kingdom of God is near.

Go lightly
        he said
        no money bag
        no sack of clothes
        and sandals one pair will do
        for nothing must distract you
        from what you have been sent to say

The kingdom of God is near.

And the crowds that come
        to hear you speak will want to know
        what are the signs
        of the kingdom's approach.

These are the signs
        you'll say
        when words become deeds

and the tables of the poor
are covered with food

when those who ought will stop
to listen and hear what you have to say
when all that is living becomes you
            and
when the cold steel of swords
melts in the fire of your love.

When this happens
        you will know
        that what you had been sent to do
        has been done
                . . . . and the kingdom of God is at hand.

your prayer is constant

"Blessed is the servant the Lord
finds watching when he comes."

Attentiveness is a common
theme in the teaching of Jesus.

He talks about staying awake,
prepared to behold
the wonders of nature,
attending to everything carefully,
pausing to study the anatomy
of a pine tree
and to catch the music
in the caw of a crow.

Creation is the work of the Lord
and its appreciation
is a constant prayer.